The Teen Girl's Gotta-Have-It Guide™ to
embarrassing
moments

How to Survive Life's Cringe-Worthy Situations!

By Jessica Blatt

Illustrated by Cynthia Frenette

Watson-Guptill Publications/New York

Senior Acquisitions Editor: Julie Mazur
Editor: Cathy Hennessy
Designer: Margo Mooney
Production Manager: Katherine Happ

First published in 2007 by Watson-Guptill Publications,
a division of VNU Business Media, Inc.
770 Broadway, New York, NY 10003
www.wgpub.com

Library of Congress Cataloging-in-Publication Data
Blatt, Jessica.
   The girl's gotta have it guide to embarrassing moments : how to
survive life's cringe-worthy situations! / Jessica Blatt ; Illustrated by
Cynthia Frenette.
        p. cm.
   Includes index.
   ISBN-13: 978-0-8230-1724-9 (alk. paper)
   ISBN-10: 0-8230-1724-9 (alk. paper)
1. Embarrassment in adolescence. 2. Teenage girls—Psychology. I. Frenette,
Cynthia. II. Title.
   BF724.3.E45B55 2007
   646.7'08352—dc22

2006023027

Printed in China

First printing, 2007

1 2 3 4 5 6 7 8 9 / 15 14 13 12 11 10 09 08 07

For Mommy,
DaDa, Stacy,
& Michele——
for getting me
through *my* most
embarrassing
moments, and for
teaching me
that, "If you can't
dazzle them with
brilliance, baffle
them with baloney."
I love you!

conte

nts

introduction

When it comes to embarrassing moments, don't you sometimes wish that life came with a rewind button?

Or that you could make the ground swallow you up?

Or that you could erase time?

Well, you're not alone. Because the thing about embarrassing moments is that they're agonizing—but they happen to *everyone.* The Queen of England! The President of the United States! That guy you've had a crush on for as long as you can remember! *Every single person* in the world has been caught in a less-than-flattering situation.

And yet, when something wretchedly blush-worthy happens to *you,* none of that seems to matter, right? It still feels like the whole world is watching you— or that for the rest of your life, everyone will think of you as the girl who tripped down a flight of stairs or farted in class or lost her bikini top at that pool party.

Well, that's where this book comes in: *The Girl's Gotta-Have-it Guide to Embarrassing Moments* is your secret weapon for dealing with the blush-fests *everyone* faces. And while it won't make cringe-worthy situations go away forever, it *will* help you survive them in style.

Dreading the Worst

Getting over embarrassing moments doesn't involve magic spells or wands. But it does involve some work on your part. See, the first step to dealing with blush-fests is to think of the *worst* ones you can imagine—and to face what's so dreadful about them. Maybe just the *thought* of getting your period in white pants keeps you up at night. But have you ever stopped to think about *why* you fear it so much? Is it because you're afraid boys will be grossed out? Or your friends will think you're not grown-up enough to handle your period coolly? Or your dad might find out you're no longer the little girl he still thinks you are?

Everyone worries about different embarrassing situations—and for different reasons. So use the next page to write down the five embarrassing situations *you* dread most—and why they freak you out, too. (And don't be shy on these pages: Think of them as a diary where you can say, do, and try out *anything,* okay?)

Top five most **embarrassing situations** that could happen (or have happened) to me— and why they're so scary:

SITUATION 1:

_____

_____

_____

SITUATION 2:

_____

_____

_____

SITUATION 3:

_____

_____

_____

SITUATION 4:

_____

_____

_____

SITUATION 5:

_____

_____

_____

The Good News

As you go through this book, you'll see how the **tricks**, **tips**, and **advice** here apply to *your* situations. You'll learn quickie-fixes, get some "one-liners" to leave 'em laughing, and find out about longer-term solutions, too.

And, even *better*: Now that you've stopped to think about the *whys* behind the embarrassing moments you dread most, you'll be better able to take control of them, too. It's a two-part process: First you have to face that, say, you're scared of striking out in front of everyone in gym class. Then you can start thinking about ways to avoid feeling so bad about it—like by devoting time to an activity that you do well and love and that will help you build your confidence.

Which brings us to another little exercise: On the next page, take a few seconds to jot down the things you *love* about yourself and that make you feel proud. They can be anything—from your perfect handwriting to your amazing sock collection to the other language you speak or your good manners. It may sound or feel corny, but when you're mindful of your strengths, you'll be less likely to feel weak when faced with embarrassing situations.

Things I Love About . . . Me!

After you fill out this page, make it a habit to say one positive thing about yourself *every* day. You can write it in your journal or say it in the shower or think it to yourself—but whichever way you choose, from this day forward, start consciously admiring yourself!

Dear diary,
I *so*
Rock!

What's Your Personality Type?

Getting through embarrassing moments doesn't mean acting like someone else or changing your identity. In fact, the best way to get over an embarrassing situation is with a strategy that feels comfortable for *you*. And the only way to find that is to learn a little bit about your personality. So bust out your pen again and take this personality pop quiz.

Mark the answer that best describes you and then follow the directions on page 12. (No peeking!)

Your friends love you because you can be counted on:	
1. To crack everyone up.	
2. To lend a listening ear.	
For your birthday, you'd love it if your parents:	
1. Threw you a surprise party.	
2. Took you and your closest friends out for a nice dinner.	
You like to dress:	
1. In flashy outfits that your friends will compliment.	
2. In simple, classic looks that feel comfortable.	
At a school dance, you can be found:	
1. Dancing, of course.	
2. Talking with friends, off to the side.	
When a teacher calls on you in class, you:	
1. Respond without a second thought.	
2. Blush, even though you know the answer.	
In group projects at school, you're the one who:	
1. Does the final presentation.	
2. Does the thorough research and preparation.	
For school parties, you:	
1. Invent a new flavor of spicy green salsa.	
2. Bake standard choco-chip cookies.	

check your score on page 12

SCORING

Now tally up your score and read on. And remember—there's no "better" or "right" answer.

If you had mostly 1s: You're an extrovert—in most situations, you're outgoing and you enjoy being the center of attention. So, when you're faced with an embarrassing situation, don't shy away from it—use your charm, sense of humor, and confidence to lessen the damage. And as you go through the solutions in this book, take time to put your peppy spin on them. Don't feel like you have to play the part of the wallflower if it's more your style to call attention to a blunder, but also remember that you don't have to make a scene over *every* little slip-up. Sometimes, playing things down really *is* the best strategy!

If you had mostly 2s: You're an introvert—you feel most comfortable in small groups, and to outsiders who don't know you well, you may seem shy. When you're faced with an embarrassing situation, channel your well of calmness and don't forget that as awkward as it can be to open up about embarrassing stuff, it *can* make you feel better to share what's going on with people you trust. As you go through the solutions in this book, remember that you don't have to force yourself to make a joke out of *every* faux pas—but that, sometimes, if you're light-hearted and casual about an embarrassing moment, others will be more likely to be casual about it, too.

The Girl's Gotta-Have-It RULES for Dealing With Embarrassing Situations AKA: S.P.R.I.N.T.!

No matter *what* your personality is, there are six golden rules for handling all embarrassing situations. Commit them to memory, or copy them down in your journal or on a piece of paper to hang in your locker!

STOP The next time you're caught in an embarrassing situation, *pause* and take a deep breath. (When you rush to react, things *always* seem worse than they really are.)

be PATIENT As with a lot of things in life, time *does* heal; embarrassing moments often look a lot less scary from the distance of even a few weeks.

REACH out Sure, you want as few people as possible in on your embarrassing moments, but *trusted* family and friends can talk you through and help you out of most situations.

be INVOLVED When you have a passion or hobby that you really care about, it's *always* there for you to throw yourself into when times get tough.

be NICE Never wiggle out of an embarrassing situation at someone else's expense—the regret you'll feel later will be worse than the shame you were trying to avoid in the first place.

be TRUTHFUL A lie may *seem* to save the day in the heat of the moment, but it will only cause drama later.

Now that you're all warmed up—you know the kinds of things you're up against and the general rules for dealing with them—let's get started tackling these embarrassing buggers!

family

fiascoes

Family is a funny thing.

On the one hand, you know with every bone of your body that there's no one who loves or cares about you more than your family. But sometimes—no matter *how* guilty it makes you feel—you can't help but want to undo the things they say or do.

And you know what? Feeling that way is perfectly normal. You don't have to beat yourself up for wanting to disappear each time your dad comes to pick you up in his clunky car or your mom wears a crazy outfit to one of your recitals or your brother gets in trouble at school—*again*—and everyone finds out.

But as normal as it is to feel embarrassed in family situations, they can be tricky to deal with because you feel torn between being loyal to the amazing family that loves you—and being true to the individual you've become and the ways that you're *different* from your family.

So what's a girl to do? Turn the page and find out!

Can't Live With 'Em, Can't Live Without 'Em

For starters, you need to clear your head. So on this page, write down the initials of everyone in your family and your other favorite relatives. Next to each set of initials, write down the one thing they embarrass you *most* by doing—like calling you "Stinky" in public or wearing bright white sunblock down their nose at the beach.

Then, after each embarrassing trait, list the three things you *love* most about each person. (And remember: You don't *have* to list something embarrassing for everyone—if you can't think of anything, just consider yourself lucky!)

INITIALS:

I get annoyed when he/she:

I love:

INITIALS:

I get annoyed when he/she:

I love:

INITIALS:

I get annoyed when he/she:

I love:

INITIALS:

I get annoyed when he/she:

I love:

INITIALS:

I get annoyed when he/she:

I love:

Look at your list and memorize it. Because the next time you're stressed about embarrassing family moments, you'll stay calm if you remind yourself that no matter how much you sometimes wish you weren't related to them, there are tons of things worth *loving* about everyone in your family. Focus on those *good* things before you react—that way, you'll be fairer and more likely to come to a resolution that makes you happy.

Now that you've focused on the good stuff but admitted what the bad stuff is, you're ready to find out how to deal with the nitty-gritty.

situation: Your little sister reveals something private about you in front of your friends—like how you wet the bed for years or still suck your thumb sometimes.

solution: Don't get mad at your sis in public—that will only call attention to the secret she spilled. Instead, consider making a joke out of whatever she revealed, by exaggerating it to the point of humor.

Did she say something about the pillow you used to practice kissing on? Come back with a line like, "Oh, yeah, I practically wanted to *marry* that pillow!" Or if she mentions that time you stuffed your bra, say, "You know you loved my Dolly Parton impersonation!" If you're not feeling particularly bold, play it down. Say, "Oh, come on, every girl in real life and TV since the beginning of time has stuffed her bra," then change the subject. Your humor will minimize the damage—and also put your friends at ease with their own embarrassing secrets. (In private, tell your sister that it hurts your feelings when she spills private things from the past. Ask her to put herself in your shoes—and she'll *quickly* understand where you're coming from!)

situation: Instead of pointing out a piece of dirt on your cheek, your mom licks her finger and rubs it off—in front of all of your friends.

solution: You'll be tempted to snap at your mom, but remember, her intentions are good. So instead, grin and bear it, then turn to your friends and ask them if they ever feel like a baby kitten around *their* moms, too. Or ham it up and give your mom a big, wet, thank you kiss in return.

leave 'em laughing

"You know the expression 'a face only a mother could love'? I guess I have a face only a mother could *eat*!"

situation: Instead of waiting in her car (like all the other moms), your mom *knocks on the door* to pick you up from a friend's house!

solution: Turn to your mom and say, "Hey, thanks for picking me up; I'm just going to get my stuff and say my thank-yous, and I'll meet you in the car." Then, when you're alone in the car with her, say, "Mom, I really appreciate you taking the time to come and pick me up—but it sort of makes me feel like a baby when you come to the door to get me. Would you mind waiting in the car next time? I promise I won't keep you waiting!"

leave 'em laughing

"How lucky am I to have a chauffeur!"

situation: Your parents show up for one of your school events either way overdressed or way underdressed.

solution: For now, grin and bear it—don't call attention to it in front of other people or during the event at all. But the next time a school event comes up, give your parents a description of *exactly* what it will be—including the dress code.

The most important thing to remember is that just having your parents' support at events is what really matters. And, sometimes, holding your tongue to spare their feelings is the best way to show your appreciation for that support.

situation: Your brother tells his hot best friend that you have a crush on him!

solution: Whether it's true or not—he *is* cute after all—the best way to handle a situation like this is to avoid overreacting. So if you enter the kitchen to get a snack and your brother turns to his friend and says, "Jake, Amy is so in love with you!" don't get all huffy and defensive. Do smile sweetly and retort with a short comment like, "Someone's being dramatic today!" grab your cookies, and walk right back out of the kitchen.

And remember, actions speak louder than words: If you're not blushing and rushing out of there, very quietly look your brother in the eye, cock your head, and simply say, "Hmph," as if you're studying something about him that he can't see. It will quickly turn the spotlight off of you and onto him. Then roll your eyes, say, "See ya," to his friend, and walk out of the room.

situation: You're out shopping with your mom when she yells your family pet name across the store to get your attention.

solution: Wave your hand so that she'll see you without *you* having to yell back across the store. Then, on the car ride home, tell her that you think it would be fun if you two came up with a whistle to find each other when you're in public places— instead of screaming out for each other. It'll be more discreet, and it will be the kind of bonding thing that becomes an inside joke with your family.

situation: Your friends come to your house—and it's a total mess.

solution: Take a deep breath and explain to your friends that your family is due for some "spring cleaning." Then bring them—and some snacks—to the most out-of-the-way part of your house, while you excuse yourself to quickly straighten up your room. (Hint: For a quick fix, throw everything from your floor into one garbage bag and slide it under your bed or into your closet.) Once you've created an open, calm space, bring your friends into it and hang out there.

Of course, if the weather's nice, you can avoid all the drama by spending the time outside!

leave 'em laughing

"Welcome to the Taj Majal, girls!"

situation: Your parents brag about you to all of their friends—while you're in the room!

solution: Keep quiet—for now. Snapping at your parents will make you and your parents feel bad and make the other people in the room feel uncomfortable. But later, in private, tell your parents that it makes you feel weird. Say, "I'm so lucky that you guys appreciate me so much—but it makes me self-conscious when you brag about me while I'm in the room, like we're being showoffs or something."

leave 'em laughing

"Do you guys want to be my personal fan club presidents?!"

situation: You walk in on your grandpa while he's going to the bathroom!

solution: Back out, close the door, and yell, "I'm sorry!" To make a joke of it—or, at the very least, to prevent it from happening again—make your own "Do Not Enter" doorknob sign, like the ones hotels use to signal whether your room is ready to be cleaned. Take a piece of construction paper, and make a hole at the top that's big enough to fit around the doorknob. Then, on one side, write something witty that conveys that the bathroom is free; on the other, write something clever that says it's in use. Some ideas: Stop!/Go!; Occupied/Vacant; Serious Business Being Conducted Inside/Recess; Court In Session/Adjourned . . . or anything else that makes you laugh and won't offend everyone else in your house!

situation: Your dad is walking around the house in his grubby undershirt—while your friends are at your house!

solution: Don't make fun of your dad in front of your friends—it will make you both feel bad. Instead, distract your friends from his outfit by leading your friends to a different room or talking to them.

Once your friends leave, you can work on getting Pops an undershirt update. Start by approaching Dad—or the person who does your dad's shopping, if it's not him. Then tell him that you love him and that you'd love him no matter *what* he wore—but that, in front of guests, it would make you feel a lot more comfortable if he'd cover up more or wear shirts that don't look like they're due for a wash. Your dad may be offended or think that you're lecturing him; if so, repeat that you know it's what's on the *inside* that counts and that he probably thinks you're being silly or superficial, but that it just makes you uneasy when your friends see this "intimate" version of him. Then offer to pick up a pack of undershirts for him the next time you're out shopping.

A FINAL NOTE

When it comes to families, sure, sometimes you just wish you could put a big "do not disturb" sign on your forehead—for a few *years*. But as you deal with your family's fiascoes, remember this:

Every family has *some* level of drama going on.
Even families that seem "perfect" on the
outside have embarrassing stories. So don't
hold your family up to an impossible standard
or expect them to never embarrass you.
Cut them—and *yourself*—some slack.

school

slip-ups

From phys ed to physics, embarrassment can feel like it's lurking in every hallway and classroom. So how's a girl supposed to get through school without losing her cool?

One way to lessen the fear of something horrifying happening is to find confidence in something you really like and can feel in control of at school. So, even if you worry about not knowing the answers in your math class, you can excel at something you enjoy—like sports or dance or art or music or writing—and become known for something positive.

See, every school—private, public, big, or small—has a ton of resources for you; the secret is to find the ones that can make your school experience more fun. There are sports teams and art clubs and language groups and bands and choirs and plays and school newspapers. And, even better, if there's something your school *doesn't* have that you wish it did—like a poetry slam club or a business class or a fencing team—*you* can be the one to talk to your school principal about starting it!

There's no denying that school is filled with embarrassing moments. But if you use your school as a tool to do something you *want* to do, you'll find the confidence to beat those moments. And you'll start looking forward to Mondays—instead of getting Sunday-night stomach-knots!

You're The Best

Making the Most of Your School Day

So how are *you* going to take control of your school day? By figuring out what your passions and talents are—and finding a way to express them.

It can feel like your school only offers a few options, but chances are, there are clubs you didn't even know existed—and if you can't find what you want, *you* can start it yourself!

If you like **WRITING**, consider joining or starting: A school newspaper, a school poetry journal, or a writing workshop

If you like **READING**, consider joining or starting: A book club, a book blog or an author visit program

If you like **COMICS**, consider joining or starting: A comic club or a comic swap

If you like **MOVIES & TV**, consider joining or starting: A movie club or a filmmaking club

If you like **DANCE**, consider joining or starting: A dance club or a dance studio for younger kids

If you like **SPORTS**, consider joining or starting: A sports column, a sports announcing program, a junior varsity or varsity team, an intramural team, a coed team, or a charity team

If you like **FOOD**, consider joining or starting: A cooking club or a cookbook-making club

If you like **ORGANIZING EVENTS**, consider joining or starting: A charity/fundraiser or a school dance

If you like **MUSIC**, consider joining or starting: A band, a charity concert, or a music-swapping club

If you like **TRAVELING**, consider joining or starting: A teen travel guidebook to your town, a school trip to a foreign country, or a student-exchange program

If you like **POLITICS**, consider joining or starting: A school trip to your state capital, a school trip to Washington, DC, a young politicians club, Student Council, Model UN, Model Congress

If you like **MAKEUP**, consider joining or starting: A club that gives makeovers to women in nursing homes or a makeup sales club

If you like **CARS**, consider joining or starting: A charity car wash or an auto show

If you like **ENVIRONMENTAL ISSUES**, consider joining or starting: An environmentalist club, an Earth Day celebration at your school or in your town, or a recycling program

If you like **TAKING PICTURES**, consider joining or starting: The yearbook, a photo class, or a photojournalism workshop

See, you can start a business club or a farming team or a languages workshop or a jewelry-making group or a perfume-swap or a fashion club or charity fashion show program or *anything* that interests you.

Not sure how to get started? First talk to a guidance counselor to see whether such a program or club exists. If it doesn't, ask the counselor about the steps you'd need to take to make it happen at your school. Chances are, there's a teacher who'd be willing to help you get your program off the ground!

Of course, even the most involved and most confident students still face some heated moments. So while you're getting ready to launch your "Young Billionaires Club," the following tips will help you cope, from homeroom to homework.

situation: Your yearbook just came out—and you *hate* your picture!

solution: Yearbook photos can feel like death sentences—like they'll always haunt you and that they forever capture a moment in history. But the truth is, *most* people hate their yearbook pictures. (That's why school picture companies offer so many special features, like "retouching" and fancy backgrounds.) So while you may want to run around school cutting out your photo from every single book, tell yourself the following: No one expects you to look like a supermodel in your class picture and, more important, after a few weeks, most people don't even *look* at their yearbooks anymore! It's unlikely that anyone will say anything to you about it, but if they do, be honest: Say, "Oh, I wish there were do-overs when it came to school pics. There's always next year!" You'll show that you're not a target to be made fun of—you know the picture isn't your finest, but you're also too cool to really let it get to you.

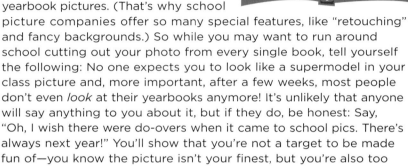

Next year, give yourself a few days to prepare for class pictures: Pick out a shirt that makes you feel confident and go ahead and practice your best smile in front of the ol' bathroom mirror. And instead of experimenting with new makeup for the first time on picture day, consider getting a free makeover at a department store cosmetic counter the weekend before picture day; you'll learn what looks are right for you, and you can even buy less expensive drugstore versions of the products the store uses. But remember: Before your makeover, find out the store's policy and make sure you won't *have* to buy anything.

leave 'em laughing

"Like my mug shot?"

situation: You get stuck in a lunch period that none of your friends are in—and you dread the idea of eating alone.

solution: Lunchroom survival just takes a little bit of pre-planning. If you're feeling bold, you can ask around your classes to find out who else has your lunch period, then flat-out ask someone you don't usually hang out with if you can join them.

But if the thought of doing that makes you feel like you'd be an annoying tag-along, here's what to do instead: On the first day of your new lunch schedule, plan your lunch carefully—make sure there's at least one item you need to buy at school and one item you can bring to share. So even if you're bringing your favorite peanut butter and banana sandwich, plan ahead to buy a drink, and to have a bag with more than enough pretzels or Gummy Bears to go around. Then use the time while you're in line buying your drink to scope out who else is in the lunchroom—and who you'd feel most comfortable approaching. Maybe you'll spy a friend you haven't seen since kindergarten. Maybe you'll see a family friend? Maybe that new girl from your science class will be sitting alone, looking like she could use some company? Look for someone you have something in common with who's not immersed in a
continued

conversation with a big group of people. Approach him or her and say, "Hey, is it okay with you if I plop down here today?" Chances are, they won't say no, and once you're sitting with someone, you'll already start to feel more at ease. From there, don't feel like you have to talk nonstop to avoid awkwardness—ask a few questions, offer to share a snack, and enjoy the company you've found. At the very best, you'll have found a new lunch buddy; at the worst, you'll have realized that looking for someone to eat with isn't so terrifying after all. (And if the first person you do approach says the seat next to him or her is taken or makes you feel weird for asking, take a deep breath and try someone on the complete opposite side of the cafeteria.)

And if you reach a point where you *really* can't stand approaching new people, consider asking a teacher or principal if you can start an ungraded lunch-time workshop—like a painting class or an arts program—that will give you a break from classes (and time to eat) but will have more structure than a free lunch period.

situation: A teacher calls on you in class, and you have *no* idea what the answer is.

solution: Whether you were too busy daydreaming or you're just unsure of the answer, get the situation over with as quickly as possible. Don't prolong it by saying nothing or pretending to be working it out. Just say, "I don't know—I need to work on this stuff/read more about it at home later." That should give your teacher the signal to call on someone else.

Then, after class, take the time to stop by your teacher's desk to address what happened and either to ask for extra help or to make clear that you'll be more focused on your work in the future. Try something like, "I've been having a hard time figuring out this chapter in our math book. Is there an online workbook or anything else you'd suggest I do to catch up?" or, "I'm sorry I wasn't prepared when you called on me. I'll be catching up on my reading tonight."

Either way, you'll have sailed through the situation *and* shown your teacher that you're super-mature—and not the kind of target she'll have to start picking on to make an example for other students.

situation: All of your friends made the cut for tryouts (for sports, for band, for the school play . . . whatever)—except for you.

solution: Getting cut from a team or activity you're interested in can be embarrassing—and stressful. It can also make you angry that you were overlooked or insecure that your friends are going to share something cool without you. So the best thing to do is to throw yourself into *another* activity—a club, or a personal project, or an after-school job. But you should also go out of your way to create opportunities to still hang out with your friends. Invite everyone over for a movie marathon, or plan a "just because" party. You'll see that you don't need to do *everything* with your friends to stay close—and that, sometimes, doing your *own* thing can make the time you spend together even more special.

solution: Whether you simply mispronounce a word or freeze completely, the best thing you can do when you're in the middle of a public speaking project is . . . *finish*. You may *want* to stop mid-sentence and run to the bathroom or back to your desk, but force yourself to march on. Take a deep breath, look at the clock in the back of the room or the one friend who you know will send you good vibes, and get the job done. Even if you have to cut things short, you'll lessen the drama of your mishap by giving it closure. If you need to buy some time, feel free to be honest with your audience—say, "Whoa, this public speaking thing looks a lot easier than it is." After class, talk to your teacher about how you can get more experience speaking in public.

leave 'em laughing

"Guess that trick about picturing everyone in their underwear doesn't work!"

situation: A school dance is coming up, and all of your friends have been asked on dates— except for you.

solution: You have a few options here, and they all involve you going after what you want instead of waiting for it to come to you. So if the dance is something you want to go to—with a date— think of a guy friend you feel comfortable being around. Maybe it's your study buddy from history class, or the neighbor you take tennis lessons with? (It doesn't *have* to be someone from your school.)

Once you decide, be brave: Don't e-mail, IM, or text him, but don't feel like you have to ask in person, either. Just call after dinner and say, "So I have this school dance next week, and a bunch of my friends are going, and I was wondering if you'd go with me/us?" If he says yes, just say, "Good. I think we'll have fun." Then, give him the details about where and when it is. If he says no, don't force the issue. Just say, "That's cool. Maybe some other time." Then, feel free to ask another guy. And remember: Sometimes, the most fun date a girl can have is her best friend—next year, maybe you and your crew can all go together *without* dates!

situation: Your team was counting on you, but you struck out.

solution: Everyone strikes out—or drops the ball, or shoots an air ball—sometimes. And even if your error costs your team the game, people *will* get over it. But the best way for *you* to get over it is to stop avoiding the field again. You may *think* that laying low will take people's minds off of your fumble, but get out there to practice like crazy, and then hustle your buns off the next time you're faced with a game. Hard work is the best way to show that you're committed to your sport—and that if it were up to you, of course you wouldn't have bobbled the ball last time.

leave 'em laughing

"Guess the Yankees won't be recruiting me this year . . ."

situation: You were in charge of the food for a school activity—and everything got burnt or turned out gross.

solution:

Okay, Grillmaster: If you were cooking meat, chicken, or anything that could actually make people sick, tell everyone to toss their plates. But if you just burnt some cookies around the edges or put a wee bit too much mustard on some sandwiches, do whatever you can to salvage them. Scrape the burnt part from the cookies, soak up some of the mustard with a paper towel, and add some extra lettuce to a salad that has too much dressing. When it comes to food, think about how you can either *add more* of something—or *take some away*—to quickly and conveniently save the day.

leave 'em laughing

"Where's Emeril when you need him?"

situation: You accidentally left your brown-bag lunch in your locker over the weekend—and now everyone is calling you "Fishy" because of the nasty smell!

solution: First, take everything out of your locker. Bring home and wash any clothes that might smell, and re-cover any textbooks that might still have the stench. Then, pick up an air freshening spray and spray it in your locker. As a final touch, tape a car air freshener (like one of those pine trees!) to the inside of your locker. And the next time you bring lunch, consider using a plastic bag that has a zipper-type lock; that way, if you accidentally leave your tuna melt or sardine sandwich overnight again, everyone won't find out!

leave 'em laughing

"Smells like something *died* in my locker!"

situation: You're chewing on your pen when—*ewww!!!*—the ink explodes all over you!

solution: Head to the school nurse's office to rinse your mouth with water, mouthwash, or any other products the nurse might have. Most pen-ink will wash off your skin with some warm water and soap.

When you get home, don't just throw your inky clothes into the hamper—let whoever does your laundry know about the stain, so that they can wash your clothes with other dark ones and avoid getting ink on anything else!

To avoid ink-spills in the future, you have two options. First, you can switch to pencils. Or, you can get yourself off the chewing habit by decorating your pen with stickers or even funky Band-Aids. Decorating your pens will give them character and discourage you from your nibbling!

leave 'em laughing

"I *gotta* stop drinking that Smurf juice."

situation: You were finally given a solo in your school's band/orchestra/play, and your instrument totally choked/your voice completely croaked.

solution: Don't stop; that will only call more attention to things. Finish your solo as quickly as possible. Then, after your performance, talk to your conductor/director/stage teacher about what happened. Ask if you can schedule some extra rehearsal time, so that you can become more familiar with your part and more comfortable on stage. Because, sometimes, even the most skilled performers just need some extra dress rehearsals.

A FINAL NOTE

There's no denying that school can be hard (and sometimes, well, really boring). But you have the power—and the right—to spice it up and get out of it what *you* want. And when you have something to look forward to at school, suddenly you'll stop thinking about the things you dread. So scribble this in your binder:

> There are certain things everyone has to face up to at school—classes, homework, social situations, tests. But you can use school to *your* advantage and seek out everything *else* it has to offer, from sports to clubs to resources like the library and guidance office. Academics may not be your strong point or social situations may make you a wee bit uncomfortable, but there really is something for everyone.

boy

bloopers

Remember when guys had cooties? Or, at least, when things with them weren't so . . . complicated?

You never *used to* care what you said in front of them or read hidden messages into everything they did, but now suddenly you're always thinking about who you like and who likes you and who's kissing who and how far she went with him or he didn't go with her.

Sometimes, the reason things get so embarrassing with a guy is because you really, really like him and don't want him to see a side of you he might not like. But, other times, even when you don't realize it, the person you're all gaga for isn't right for you anyway— *or* worth stressing out about.

So before jumping into the rules for dealing with embarrassing guy situations, it's first worth figuring out what kind of guys are *worth* your time.

SUSHI

VINTAGE

For your birthday dinner, you request...

NEW

YOUR FAVORITE PIZZA

ONE OF A KIND

The perfect formal/prom dress is one that's...

BLACK AND SIMPLE

ANY STROKES CLASSIC

ANY AMERICAN IDOL HIT FAVORITE

Your karaoke song of choice is...

Your perfect match is:

THE QUIRKY REBEL

The guy who's best for you doesn't fit into any ordinary mold. Look for guys who are as unique as you are—they'll teach you new things and fuel your curiosity!

Your perfect match is:

THE CLASSIC ROMANTIC

The guy who's best for you makes you feel comfortable and secure. Look for guys who you feel like yourself around, and who can be good friends with you, too.

Figuring out what kind of guy is best for you doesn't mean figuring out a "type" in a superficial kind of way; it means thinking about the kind of person who will make you happiest. And when he comes along, you're bound to face some of these sticky situations. So fasten your seatbelt and get ready to learn a lesson or two!

situation: Your crush walks in—while you're talking about him to your friends.

solution: Here's one embarrassing situation that you can transform into a great opportunity. Because, especially if your crush is shy, hearing from *you* that you're interested could give him more confidence to hang around you . . . which could lead to him asking you out or you asking him out. So if he walks in while you're going on and on about his amazing drawings or cute smile, end what you're saying about him, and switch the topic to something totally safe, like your favorite TV show. But even as you switch the topic, make sure to make eye contact with your crush, smile, and then turn away. Because he may not have heard exactly what you were *saying*—but a flirty smile will let him know exactly how you *feel* without putting yourself out there too much.

leave 'em laughing

"Someone's ears must've been ringing!"

solution: Act fast! As soon as you realize your mistake, send a follow-up e-mail to your crush saying, "Uh, you *do* realize that last e-mail was a joke, right? I thought it would make you laugh, but then it occurred to me that you may have thought I was serious. Sorry for the confusion!" (Yes, this is stretching the truth!) If he's not online and you don't hear from him within the next few minutes, feel free to leave him a short voicemail saying "Hey, it's ____. If you haven't checked your e-mail recently, there's one waiting from me from this morning that's a joke—just wanted to make sure you realized!" Then, call your best friend to laugh about it and promise yourself you'll *never* do that again!

solution: It can be awkward for your parents when they realize that guys come with the territory of growing up. So if they catch you being affectionate with your crush, understand that they might get angry—but that it's only because it's a change for them and something new for them to worry about. But they worry because they love you, so you need to assure them that they can relax. If your mom sees you give your crush a kiss goodbye, tell her, "Oh, I hope that wasn't weird for you to see!" Then share something else about your crush, so that your mom feels like she's part of this new world you're exploring. Tell her, "Andy's painting made it into the school art show," or "Andy and I were on opposite gym teams today, and it was so funny that I struck him out at softball." If it's your dad, you can leave out the part about the kiss and just share something about this guy that will make him feel like less of a stranger—and more like a friend your dad can trust to be hanging out with his daughter.

situation: Your crush catches you in a less-than-flattering situation—like with your underwear sticking out of your jeans or with food in your mouth.

solution: The best way to wipe out a negative impression is with a positive one. So if your Tuesday panties were sticking out from your sweats, wear your cutest and most flattering jeans or pants the *next* time you know you'll be seeing your crush. If you realize you were talking to your crush with some spinach from your veggie-pizza stuck in your teeth, don't start avoiding him— make a point of starting an interesting conversation with him the next time you see him—while looking him straight in the eye.

If you feel comfortable, you can always talk about the incident—
"By the way, I realized after lunch that I had a piece of food stuck
in my teeth that whole time—you could've told me!" But don't harp
on it, or he'll start to think about it more than he probably was in
the first place!

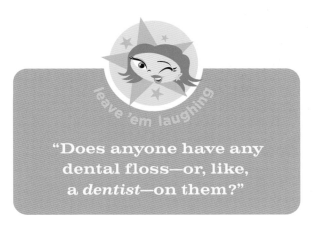

leave 'em laughing

"Does anyone have any
dental floss—or, like,
a *dentist*—on them?"

situation: Your crush leans in to give you a kiss—finally—and you realize you have bad breath!

solution: You won't want to ruin the moment you've been waiting for by asking him to hold on while you slip yourself a mint or piece of gum. But you also don't want him to never kiss you again or spread a rumor that you have dog breath! Which is why this situation is tricky. The best thing to do is to keep it short and sweet. Keep your mouth closed, and if you're feeling comfortable, shift the focus from lips-on-lips to give him an affectionate peck on his cheek, nose, or forehead. Remember: If he really likes you and you're meant to be together, there will be other opportunities for fresh-breath smooching in the future!

To ward off bad breath in the future, always carry (sugar-free) gum or mints with you. Brush your teeth at least twice a day, and don't forget to brush your *tongue* with your toothbrush, too!

"I gotta lay off the garlic gum!"

A FINAL NOTE

Having a crush is like learning to knit—when things go well, you can create something awesome that you want to take with you everywhere. But there are lots of times when you can get stuck—and mildly hurt. So remember the following:

Guys are people too. They're not gods. And any one of 'em who expects you to be flawless and a perfect angel or doesn't have a sense of humor about the human things we *all* do— well, he just isn't worth your time.

body

blunders

When you were a baby, you—like *everyone else* out there—wore diapers. You pooped whenever you felt like it, wet the bed constantly, and were *encouraged* to spit up.

But, my, how things change! The older you get, the more it can feel like your bodily functions are secrets you'd rather bury than celebrations you want to share with the whole world. Some days, it can even feel like your own body is ganging up on you—sprouting unwanted hair or smells, and growing and changing faster than you can say *wheredidthatcomefrom?!*

The good news is that you're not the first—or only person—to have to deal with the dreaded P-word: Puberty. And like the bazillions of girls before you, you can deal with even the most awkward body drama—with a little planning and the tips in this chapter.

How Well Do You *Really* Know Your Body?

The more you know about what's going on inside your body, the more comfortable you'll be in your own skin. So mark "T" next to each statement you think is true and "F" next to each statement you think is false. Then check your answers on page 54.

TRUE or FALSE?

1.	Everyone's left and right breasts are the same size.	
2.	Chocolate causes pimples.	
3.	Talking on the phone can give you acne.	
4.	You should get your period every 28 days.	
5.	Girls and guys fart the same amount.	
6.	Deodorant prevents sweating.	
7.	All vaginas look the same.	
8.	Masturbating is bad for you.	
9.	Brunettes are smarter than blondes.	
10.	The sun is good for acne.	
11.	Everyone gets pubic hair.	
12.	Dandruff only happens in dirty hair.	
13.	Using a tampon is bad for you.	
14.	You should get your period by the time you're 13.	
15.	Only guys get hair on their toes or fingers.	

see answers on page 54

solution: If you really can't put your shoes back on, do whatever you can to discreetly move them as far away as possible from everyone else—to the other side of the room or in your locker—without getting in trouble. If anyone asks why you're not keeping your sneakers with the rest of the group's, just shrug, smile, and say you might have stepped in something "funky" earlier in the day—and you don't want to junk up everyone else's shoes. By being vague, you won't be lying—and you'll have avoided anyone discovering the truth. (PS: When you get home, ask a parent if you can put your sneakers in the washing machine to freshen them up. Otherwise, try tucking dryer sheets in them overnight.)

leave 'em laughing

"Don't call 'em sneakers— call 'em *stinkers!*"

QUIZ ANSWERS

Now, take a look at the answers, and remember the most important lesson of all about your body: No matter how frustrated you may get with it, it's a beautiful, wonderful, amazingly complex *gift* that you should take good care of—and *not* take for granted.

1. Everyone's left and right breasts are the same size. FALSE

Not only are no two pairs of breasts alike, but almost everyone has one breast that's larger or shaped differently than the other one.

2. Chocolate causes pimples. FALSE

There's no proven connection between eating chocolate and getting acne. But there's also no arguing with the fact that eating fresh fruit and vegetables and drinking water is a great way to keep your skin glowing, from the inside out.

3. Talking on the phone can give you acne. TRUE

No, gossiping doesn't cause acne! But pressing the phone against your jaw or chin can irritate your skin or trap dirt and oil inside your pores. So consider using a hands-free device on your cell or the "speaker" option on your home phone. And every so often, clean your phone with an astringent.

4. You should get your period every 28 days. FALSE

Everyone's period is different—especially when you first start getting it. Some girls have their period for just a few days, while others have it for a full week. And while 28 days is a common cycle, it's not abnormal if yours falls a little bit shorter or longer. Of course, if your periods are painful or last so long that they make you uncomfortable, tell your doctor.

5. Girls and guys fart the same amount. TRUE

Guys may talk about farting more, but *everyone* passes about the same amount of gas!

6. Deodorant prevents sweating. FALSE

Deodorant is like perfume for your armpits—it just makes you smell like whatever scent it's labeled as. Your deodorant will only keep you from sweating if it's also an *antiperspirant*.

7. All vaginas look the same. FALSE

The analogy is corny, but true: Vaginas are like snowflakes, and no two are the same. But, again, if you're worried about the way yours looks, ask your pediatrician or gynecologist about it. They'll be able to discuss your specific concerns with you.

8. Masturbating is bad for you. FALSE

In the "olden days," people used to think that masturbating could make you blind! But these days, we know that masturbating is a normal, healthy habit for guys *and* girls.

9. Brunettes are smarter than blondes. FALSE

Blondes don't have more fun and brunettes aren't any smarter than redheads or blondes or anyone else! There's simply no connection between brainpower and hair color.

10. The sun is good for acne. FALSE

You may think that a day at the beach is clearing up your acne, but the sun can actually do more long-term damage to your skin than be any good for it. So make sure you cover your skin with sunblock every time you'll be outside.

continued

11. Everyone gets pubic hair. TRUE

After going through puberty, everyone—of each gender and every race, religion, and background—grows pubic hair. So you're not alone. And for any hair that truly bothers you, there's always a safe way to remove it—from waxing to shaving to electrolysis and laser removal, so don't let it keep you down!

12. Dandruff only happens in dirty hair. FALSE

Even the cleanest hair can develop white, flaky dandruff. The best thing to do if you think you have dandruff is to consult a dermatologist—she'll be able to rule out any other possible scalp conditions and can give you a prescription shampoo or direct you to an over-the-counter treatment that will be right for you.

13. Using a tampon is bad for you. FALSE

Tampons are safe—as long as you read the directions on the box and change yours regularly.

14. You should get your period by the time you're 13. FALSE

There's no "exact" age that you should get your period. Some girls get their period in elementary school, while others don't get it until high school. But whether you're an early bloomer or a late bloomer, know that you can and should talk to your doctor about any concerns or discomfort you may be feeling.

15. Only guys get hair on their toes or fingers. FALSE

You may think you're weird for sprouting hair on places like your toes, fingers, or belly, but rest assured that tons of girls get hair in places they'd rather they didn't! The good news is that there are lots of safe, affordable ways to remove unwanted hair; talk to a dermatologist about the way that's best for your skin type. If you don't have a dermatologist, you can always ask your pediatrician.

Everyone's bodies are different—what's "normal" for some people may not be normal for others. And if you're ever concerned about body stuff, feel free to ask your doctor or school nurse about it. That's what they're there for!

situation: You got your period unexpectedly—and it seeped through your jeans!

solution: If you can't go home to change, grab a sweatshirt or jacket to tie around your waist. Can't find one? Just make sure your backpack or book bag hangs low enough on your butt to cover the stain. And if that's not an option, find something *else* to intentionally stain your pants with—like salad dressing, mustard, chocolate, paint, or ink, if you're near supplies. That way, if anyone comments on your butt, you can say you spilled one of those less embarrassing items on yourself instead.

Once you get home, run cold water directly over the stain; then ask one of your parents what kind of stain removal items you have. If the stain doesn't come out, consider sewing a funky patch onto the stain and all over your pants, so it looks intentional.

And remember: Always keep spare tampons or pads in your backpack or locker, in a discreet bag or an extra pencil case. And when you do have your period, avoid wearing light colors or tight clothes. Toward the end of your period, wear a panty-liner or a lightweight pad until you're sure your period is over—sometimes it may stop for a day but then come back again.

situation: You let out a fart—and everyone hears it!

solution: This is the oldest embarrassing situation in the world—but one that never gets any less awkward. So if you're in a room with *lots* of people, don't react or say anything. Someone else might say something out loud, but you can just keep your cool and act like it's news to you, too.

Of course, if you're one of just a few people in the room and everyone knows who "dealt it," you have two options. If you're feeling bashful, *don't* acknowledge it, but start a conversation to cover for the dead silence and move on. If you're around people you know well and are feeling silly, feel free to jokingly say, "Oopsie," roll your eyes, and then move the conversation along.

Remember: Gas is only human, but you can minimize feeling gassy in public by not eating certain foods before you go out. For some people, vegetables like beans or broccoli lead to gas; for other people, it's dairy or fruit. Listen to your body and remember not to cut healthy foods out of your diet—just avoid them in moments when you're worried about being in a big group for a long stretch of time.

situation: You wake up with a monstrous zit on your face.

solution: There are a million ways to treat a zit—from over-the-counter medicines to creams, gels, and pills only a dermatologist can prescribe. But when you have just a few minutes to deal with one, the best thing to do is cover it up.

So make sure you always have these two items on hand, for zit emergencies: A liquid concealer, and pressed or loose powder. (Choose a brand that says "non-comedogenic," which means it won't clog your pores. Otherwise, the makeup can actually lead to more breakouts!)

Apply the concealer all around your zit and brush it in with a clean finger or makeup sponge. Once it's covered, dab it lightly with the powder. Then look in the mirror—if you can see the powder or it looks like dust, dab it with a dry tissue to remove the excess makeup.

Your bangs curl up like little worms whenever it's humid out.

solution: There's a reason why cheap drugstores were invented: Hair supplies! The answer to embarrassing bangs is a mini bottle of hairspray plus some barrettes. Pick out simple barrettes, like silver ones or a color that matches your hair. Then sweep your bangs back and use the barrettes to hold them in place as far back on the top of your head as they'll go. So that you don't look like Fifi the dog, use three or four squirts of hairspray to hold down fly-aways. And remember: The next time you get your hair cut, make sure to tell the stylist that your hair is wavy or curly—she'll be able to give you a cut that suits your hair type.

situation: Your hair is all staticky—and keeps standing up instead of staying down against your head!

solution: Get to the closest water fountain or sink, run your hands under the faucet, then run your hands through your hair. Or keep a dryer sheet in your backpack and run it over your dry head to tame that static electricity— you might feel funny doing it, but it works!

leave 'em laughing

"My hair's battery-charged today!"

situation: You're at a sleepover party and your period leaked onto your host's sheet or blanket.

solution: Okay, it's time to do damage control. First, change into clean underwear and clothes. Then, discreetly cover the stain with your blanket, overnight bag, or anything else you have and can "accidentally forget" at your friend's house when your ride comes to pick you up. When you get home, ask a parent to call your friend's mom in confidence. Your parent can offer to wash the sheets or buy new ones. But most moms remember when they, too, had accidents—chances are, they'll wash the sheets themselves and keep the secret to themselves.

In the meantime, survive your next sleepover by always packing a "just in case" pad or panty-liner.

situation: You're at school or a party and you realize you have body odor.

solution: It's natural to have "b.o." sometimes—everybody does. If you're out of the house when you realize you have it and you can't get to a shower or a change of clothes or perfume, head to the closest bathroom and grab three paper towels. Wet two of them. Then squeeze soap onto one of the wet ones, and rub it until it works up some suds. Go into the bathroom stall, and take off your shirt. "Sponge" your armpits with the soapy towel, "rinse" them with the wet one, and "dry" them with the third towel.

In the future, you can avoid b.o. by showering regularly (and especially after playing sports), shaving your armpits, using an antiperspirant and/or deodorant, and regularly washing your clothes. (Sometimes it's not you that smells—it's your favorite T-shirt!) Another tip: Start keeping a mini-deodorant (the travel aisle of most drug stores carries them) or mini-perfume or body spray inside your bag so you'll always have a quick fix on hand.

A FINAL NOTE

You know how, when you get new sneakers, it takes you a while to really feel comfortable in them? Well, your body is changing so much, that it's almost like you have new sneakers for every part of it! So give yourself time to get used to it and take comfort in this: Before you know it, you *will* feel good in your body. Until you get to that comfortable place, remember:

Calmness and a sense of humor go a long way when it comes to bodily functions. There's no need to call attention to an uncomfortable body moment—but if someone else does, play it down with a joke, a shrug, or a smile.

faux pas

Playing dress-up is one of those childhood games that never goes out of style.

And yet, the older you get, the more it can feel like getting dressed is more work than play! There are bra straps to worry about and low-riding jeans to squeeze into, and suddenly you feel like you can't just wear the same sweatshirt and jeans every day, like you did when you were younger.

And though it's true that what's on the inside counts more than what's on the outside, the two go hand in hand: When you're dressed in a way that makes you feel and look good, you'll be more confident and more eager to go after your goals. You'll also make the kind of first impressions you want to make and send a message to people you meet that you take pride in yourself.

So how can you make clothes work for you—and make fashion fun again?

Dream Look Collage

Looking great doesn't mean you have to choose some high-maintenance style or look. It means you should wear what makes you feel most *comfortable.*

So take your favorite old magazines and, on a separate sheet of paper, make a collage of your dream look—clothes you love, styles you want to make your own, and accessories that look cool. And remember that magazines are designed to *inspire* you, not necessarily give you a head-to-toe look you'd wear to school. So if you love, say, a vest in a magazine, but the model is wearing it over just her bra, remember that you can use the vest you love but pair it over a tank top or T-shirt or something that will make you feel more like you—and less like a flashy runway model. Or if you love a trend like beaded necklaces, but the one in the magazine is $100, use it as inspiration to buy some beads and make one on your own, or to try to find a similar version for $10 at the mall.

This project will get you thinking about how you *want* to dress— which, you might find, is way different from how you've been dressing. Keep the collage in the back of your mind—or in the front of your wallet—the next time you go shopping.

Now, while you work on making your dream looks a reality, keep the following suggestions in mind for getting through your next fashion disasters!

situation: You realize mid-conversation that your fly is open!

solution: Discreetly pull your fly up as soon as you realize. The next time you're shopping for pants, try them on both standing up and sitting down, to make sure the fly stays closed no matter what. And don't try to squeeze into jeans that are too tight—your fly will be more likely to slip down!

situation: You start sweating—and it shows through your shirt!

solution: If your girls' locker room has a hand-dryer, use it to dry the wet marks. But if not, here's the deal: If your shirt is short-sleeved, bunch your sleeves up on top of your shoulders, as if you're intentionally trying to make it look like a sleeveless shirt. If it's long-sleeved, keep your backpack on so that the straps cover it. Or throw a T-shirt over it; it will look like you're making a fashion statement, and it will hide the danger zones.

The next time you go shopping for deodorant, consider buying one that says "antiperspirant," too; that means it will not only hide odors but will also prevent the sweat that causes them.

And when the weather gets warm or you know you'll be doing something really active, remember to steer clear of shirts that turn a darker shade when they're wet—like reds, oranges, grays, and some pastels. Stick to solids in black or white.

leave 'em laughing

"Sweat marks are my hot new fashion accessory this summer!"

situation: You get to school or a party and realize you have deodorant stains on your shirt.

solution: It can totally ruin your mood or make you feel like a slob when some deodorant shows up on your shirt. The best way to get rid of a stain on fabrics like cotton and wool on the spot is *not* to use water. Instead, rub the stain out with the fabric of the shirt. (If you can slip into the bathroom to take your shirt off, rub an unstained part of your shirt against the stained part, and it should fade and disappear.) If you're near a dry terrycloth towel, you can run that along the stain and—presto—it should come out.

Another tip:
Put deodorant on *after* you get dressed. Or try a clear, gel-like deodorant to avoid stains in the future.

leave 'em laughing

"Looks like my deodorant took a little stroll down my shirt!"

situation: You show up to a party *way* under-dressed, overdressed, or . . . just dressed wrong!

solution: If there's no way for you to slip out to change into more suitable clothes, the only person you really need to say something to is your host. But don't call too much attention to your error. Simply say, "I had no idea this was wasn't a casual event; I didn't mean any disrespect by my outfit." Your host will appreciate the consideration— and (if she's a good host) make you feel better about it.

leave 'em laughing

"I'm turning *myself* over to the fashion police for this one!"

solution: Slide your bikini bottom down a little bit lower on your hips to give yourself more fabric further down. If the extra bunching of fabric still doesn't hide everything, slip back into a pair of shorts or wrap a towel around your waist.

The next time you go bathing suit shopping, consider a style that's less revealing—like a boy-short, instead of a string bikini. And remember: A painful but quick bikini wax can go a long way in boosting your self-confidence in *any* bathing suit!

situation: You wear your comfy granny-panties with jeans and then you realize everyone's looking at your visible panty line!

solution: Visible panty lines ("VPL") happen all the time. So start keeping an extra pair of less bulky undies (in a discreet brown paper bag) in your locker, for quick changes. If you're not near an extra pair to change into, there's always the option to wear no undies at all for the rest of the day.

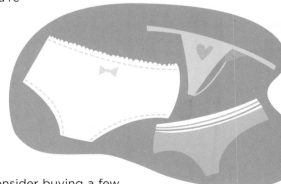

(But remember: While that solution is free, it could cost you your comfort!)

The next time you go underwear shopping, consider buying a few pairs meant specifically for tight pants and skirts.
Try a thong in a natural fabric like cotton, or even a boy short made of a thin material and with a loose enough elastic so that it doesn't create bulges at the top of your thighs.

situation: Your shirt is see-through.

solution: As with sweaty situations, throw a T-shirt on top of your shirt, if you have one on hand. Otherwise, keep your arms folded across your chest, and don't pose for any pictures—the flash has a way of revealing even *more* than you can see in regular light! And remember that even though a white bra seems like the best color to wear under a white shirt, you should actually wear a *skin*-colored bra with light tops. Pick one up the next time you're out bra shopping.

A FINAL NOTE

Embarrassing clothing moments happen to everyone, no matter what their style is. And while you can't always prevent them, you can be ready to deal with them. Here's a tip you can copy down and keep in your pocket:

> **You don't have to follow trends or spend a lot of money to feel great in the clothes you wear. Focus instead on finding clothes that look great on *you*. Because if you feel good in your outfits, you'll be more confident when it comes to handling fashion faux pas.**

travel

trauma

Vacations are supposed to be great—they're the time to stop thinking about homework, spend time with your family, and try new things. But what nobody ever seems to want to admit is that vacations can be *stressful*, too!

From packing your luggage to prancing around in your new bikini, there are tons of embarrassing situations that can crop up. This chapter is your passport to get through them.

The key to avoiding—or, at least, minimizing—embarrassing situations while on vacation is to make sure you're as relaxed as possible. Not only will a chilled-out mood make you more likely to stay calm while away from home, but finding a way to unwind will give you something positive to focus on, no matter what crops up!

How Can *You* Make the Most of Your Vacation

Your favorite exercise is . . .

YOGA → **You love guys with great . . .**

PILATES

HIKING → **Your favorite class is . . .**

ACCENTS

HISTORY

MUSIC TASTES

With your girlfriends, you love to . . .

RENT MOVIES

INVENT NEW RECIPES

GO DANCING

GYM

Your homepage is . . .

Your favorite field trip is to the . . .

MTV.COM

CNN.COM

ART MUSEUM

AQUARIUM

Nothing's more relaxing for you than being pampered or laying low. So even if your family trip is to some place active, make sure to bring along a juicy novel or magazines to unwind with at the end of each day.

You're fascinated by other cultures and learning new things. No matter what kind of trip your family plans, pack a camera and a journal so you can document and reflect on your experiences.

You love being physically active, wherever you go. So pack a sports bra and your sneakers and a parent to help you find a safe, public place to jog and explore your new surroundings.

solution:

Whoops! Unintentional flashing can make you want to cover yourself in turtlenecks and sweats for the rest of your life. But the truth is, everyone has the same body parts. And while yours usually aren't on display, there's really nothing about them that hasn't

been shown on TV, pictured in magazines, or drawn in your school textbooks. So just pull your top up, say "Whoops," smile, and hold your head up high. (And if it will make you feel better, throw a tank top over your suit for the rest of the day!)

The next time you go bathing suit shopping, look for styles with straps—like halters or T-straps. Or if you know you'll be doing something active, like swimming or water-skiing, consider wearing a bathing suit that gives you comfort *and* coverage, like a one-piece or a tankini.

leave 'em laughing

"Look, Ma, no top!"

situation: Your suitcase appears on the baggage carousel wide open—and everyone can see your panties and bras!

solution: If you're with a friend or your sister, ask her to help you round up your stuff from the conveyor belt. But if you're alone or don't have someone nearby to help, just bunch everything up in your arms, then bring your suitcase and stray clothes to a nearby bench or chair. That'll get you out of the spotlight, and also give you space to get your stuff—and *yourself*—together calmly.

The next time you're packing for a trip, group things into individual plastic bags within your suitcase—your toiletries in one bag, your bras in another bag, your laundry in its own bag, etc. It will spare you future drama—and keep your suitcase better organized.

leave 'em laughing

"Next time, I might as well just take a see-through suitcase!"

situation: You got a sunburn on your beach vacation—and now you have to go back to school looking like a bright red lobster!

solution: Ouch! Burns aren't just embarrassing—they're painful. So if yours is making you sick or has caused any kind of blisters or funny-looking freckles, show your parents; they may want to take you to your doctor or dermatologist. In the meantime, drink lots of water and use a soothing topical gel, like a lotion with aloe in it. (It might be cold on your hot skin, so rub a little bit between your hands to warm it up, before you apply it to your burn.)

The next time you travel to a sunny location, remember to pack a hat and a light T-shirt that covers the sensitive skin on your shoulders and back. If you'll be swimming, make sure your sunblock is waterproof—being in the water may cool you off, but it *doesn't* protect you from burning. Even with waterproof sunscreen, it's important to reapply often throughout the day.

And remember: You should wear sunblock *every* day—not just when you're going to the beach.

leave 'em laughing

"Did someone order a lobster?"

situation: You come home from your adventurous vacation with mosquito bites—all over your face!

solution: To get rid of the swelling, try an over-the-counter cream with cortisone in it. If the bumps stay red, use a bit of concealer and powder to cover them up. And whatever you do, resist that urge to scratch!

leave 'em laughing

"You could play connect-the-dots on my face!"

situation: A team of hot guys is staying at the same hotel as your family—but you're stuck babysitting your siblings!

solution: Chances are you're not going to have the time or opportunity to really get to know any one of the guys. But if you want to make a good impression—and maybe practice your flirting skills—the best thing to do is *not* to act embarrassed to be with your family. Go *out* of your way to be helpful and friendly and involved with your family. If you're just sitting around quietly, that's not much of an invitation for a guy to feel comfortable talking to you! But if you're helping your brother get up on his water skis or showing your sister how to switch the gears on her bike, who knows what kind of conversation might start naturally.

A FINAL NOTE

Vacations are a precious time to get a break from your routine—but sometimes the change in scenery can make you unsettled or come with a host of situations you're not expecting. So keep the following in mind the next time you're "on holiday":

See vacations as adventures: They're a chance to experience new surroundings, foods, cultures, and activities. And if you go into them with an open mind and a can-do attitude, you'll be so focused on trying new things and soaking up every ounce of fun and relaxation that you'll barely even notice mishaps!

aneous
mishaps

By this point, you've probably been able to relate to a bunch of the scenarios in the previous chapters— because *everyone* goes to school and has families and deals with puberty!

But life's filled with all kinds of embarrassing situations that don't always fall neatly into any one category. So that's where this chapter comes in—it's designed to help you get through all those random, quirky, and bizarre times when you wish you could just make yourself disappear!

situation: You're at a store register, with a long line behind you, ready to buy something, when suddenly you realize you don't have enough money.

solution: Even though everyone's been caught without enough money at one time or another, all it takes is an evil look from a cashier or a snooty laugh from the person in line behind you to make you wish you could hide in the dressing room forever. But don't beat yourself up—instead, say, "I'm so sorry, but it looks like I'll have to come back later for this." Then offer to return the item to the shelf and step aside so that the person behind you can pay instead of becoming impatient with you.

leave 'em laughing

"Looks like my money called in sick today!"

solution: Apologize. *Immediately*. Say, "Mr. Robins, I'm sorry for using that language. It won't happen again." Then, make *sure* it doesn't!

situation: You call someone you've recently been introduced to by the wrong name!

solution: Don't pretend it didn't happen. As soon as you realize, address the person by the right name, and apologize. Say, "Tracy, I'm so sorry I called you Allison before—I had my sister, Allie, on my mind, and just spaced out for a second there!" Then resume the conversation, and show a genuine interest in the person by asking them questions, looking them in the eye, and nodding along.

situation: You have an after-school job, and your crush/teacher/crush's mom comes in and you have to wait on him or her.

solution: Be a real pro—wow *whoever* it is by giving him or her the best level of service possible. Even if you have a uniform you hate or have to follow work rules that make you roll your eyes, you'll prove that you're mature, responsible, polite, and gracious. Can you think of any *more* impressive traits?

situation: You thought you hung up your cell phone, and you accidentally start talking *about* your friend while her voicemail is still recording!

solution: Don't wait for your friend to confront you—that will only drag things out and make you both more uncomfortable. Instead, call her back immediately and apologize. Tell her that you're not only embarrassed but you're also just plain ashamed for talking behind her back. Then, tell her that you'll understand if she needs some time to get over being upset with you—but that you hope she'll eventually forgive you. And *reassure* her that you won't talk about her again!

situation: You compliment someone on his or her cute baby—but assume it's a boy, when it's really a girl, or vice versa!

solution: Parents have a tendency to take that kind of comment personally, as if it's their fault there would be any mix-up, so make them realize it was *your* little mistake. Say, "I'm so sorry—I'm not around babies much, so I guess it was silly of me not to notice! But, really, she's precious."

the final exam

You've finally made it!

You've "survived" more than **50** embarrassing moments, and you now have the tools for handling pretty much anything that comes your way.

But before you *officially* cross the finish line, it's time for a little "final exam"! Flip back to page **8,** and use this page to rewrite the five most embarrassing situations you wrote about there. Then, think of all the tips and tricks you've learned throughout this book to come up with a strategy for tackling each situation on your list.

SITUATION 1:
_____

Girl's Gotta-Have-It strategy: _____

_____

_____

_____

_____

SITUATION 2:
_____

Girl's Gotta-Have-It strategy: _____

_____

_____

_____

_____

SITUATION 3:
_____

Girl's Gotta-Have-It strategy: _____

_____

_____

_____

_____

SITUATION 4:

Girl's Gotta-Have-It strategy:

_____

_____

_____

SITUATION 5:

Girl's Gotta-Have-It strategy:

_____

_____

_____

_____

A FINAL NOTE

Remember: No matter what embarrassing situation crops up in your life, you'll be able to get through it like a champ if you keep in mind these three goals:

1: Develop a sense of inner confidence about who you are by doing things you enjoy.

2: Realize that, as excruciating as it may seem sometimes, _no_ embarrassing moment is the end of the world; the things that _really_ matter most (your family, your health, your true friends) won't be affected by it.

3: Learn to laugh at yourself and trust that things always look better after a good night's sleep!

extra credit!

Now, it's time to celebrate! Because you've realized that laughing at *yourself* can help when it comes to embarrassing situations——but so can just plain *laughing*. So in this chapter it's time to have some *fun!*

Q&A

You may feel like you're the first person who has ever had to face embarrassing moments, but the fact is everyone has found themselves in a cringe-worthy situation at some point! That means that even your parents, grandparents, siblings, and friends have lived through their share of similar embarrassing situations!

So take time to "interview" your friends and family. Ask them what their most embarrassing moment was—and how they got through it. You'll learn more about your family—and you may discover a whole bunch of new tricks, too!

_____

_____

_____

_____

_____

_____

_____

_____

_____

_____

WORD SEARCH

Can you find all of these embarrassing situations in this puzzle?
Look up, down, across, diagonal—and backwards!

BAD BREATH, EMAIL DRAMA, FART IN CLASS, FOOD IN TEETH,
FRIZZY HAIR, MISSING BIKINI, MONSTER ZIT, OPEN FLY,
PERIOD STAIN, STRIKEOUT

```
T  E  E  T  I  Z  R  E  T  S  N  O  M  S  O
B  N  Y  E  M  A  I  L  D  R  A  M  A  T  P
A  I  H  T  E  E  T  N  I  D  O  O  F  A  E
D  A  P  O  M  F  O  B  A  B  R  P  A  N  E
B  T  S  I  N  L  R  N  L  I  M  E  R  N  M
R  S  T  E  N  I  K  I  I  K  P  N  T  I  O
E  D  S  T  R  I  K  K  Z  B  A  F  I  Z  N
A  O  E  N  A  T  K  E  T  Z  B  L  N  Z  T
I  I  F  O  O  J  J  L  E  H  Y  Y  C  N  T
H  R  S  C  H  Y  Z  Z  I  T  Y  H  L  I  F
P  E  R  I  O  X  F  O  O  P  R  S  A  Z  A
E  P  A  T  T  U  O  E  K  I  R  T  S  I  R
H  E  F  R  O  Z  Z  Y  O  U  T  Z  S  R  R
I  N  I  K  I  B  G  N  I  S  S  I  M  B  O
```

(answers on page 92)

What It Really Takes to be a BFF!

Part of what makes embarrassing situations so brutal is feeling like you're going through them alone. Just think how a situation that's horrific on your own (like, say, getting ink all over your clothes) would seem hilarious if it happened to you *and* your best friend.

See, there's safety and comfort in having friends to get you through embarrassing moments. Which is why it's important for *you* to know how to help a friend when she's in an awkward situation. So keep these *Girl's Gotta-Have-It* Friendship Rules in mind—because it's true that "a friend in need is a friend indeed"—and that being a good friend to others usually leads to others being good friends to *you*.

Create a distraction. Do whatever you can to call attention away from your friend and attract the attention to you!

Share the spotlight. If there's no way to shift people's stares from your friend to you, go over and join her in her mess—if she tripped and her books went flying everywhere, help her pick them up!

Zip your lips. Once the immediate moment settles down, do your best to not talk about what happened to your friend. And if someone asks you about it, play it down and say, "It was really no big deal."

Lend an ear. If a friend needs to talk to you about what happened, let her work things through with you. Reassure her that it will all pass and that whatever's happened to her has probably happened to tons of other girls just like her.

Help her help herself. Wallowing in pity is never good for a friend—or a friendship. So if a few days pass and your friend is still majorly worked up about what happened, ask her if there's anything specific you can help her with, beyond just being a good listener. Maybe she'd want to talk to your mom, instead of her own, about a situation? Maybe she'd want you to come talk to a teacher with her?

Don't strand her. As long as you attempt to do *something,* you'll be doing your duty as a friend. But don't ever just walk away. That's the most important rule, so remember it above all else.

Guilty Pleasures

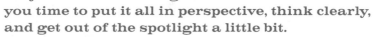

Running away from embarrassing situations won't solve them. But sometimes—especially for the majorly frustrating ones—escaping from them for just a little bit can give you time to put it all in perspective, think clearly, and get out of the spotlight a little bit.

So if you're going to take a mini-vacation from the situation, here are some fun ways to distract yourself!

Take a hike. Or a walk. Or a jog. You'll clear your head and give yourself a goal you can feel good about accomplishing.

Lend a hand. Offer to set the dinner table or help your sister with her math homework. When you focus your energy on getting someone else through something they need help with, you focus less on yourself.

Head to your room, blast your favorite song, and sing along to it! Belting out the lyrics will give you an outlet for all that nervous energy.

Read. Getting lost in a story will distract you from your own story.

Give yourself an at-home manicure / pedicure. The concentration it takes to paint ten fingers and ten toes will distract you from you-know-what.

Time Capsule

Time really *does* heal all—which is why the things that make you cringe now might make you laugh later...or at least make you realize how much you've changed or grown up.

So to see how much you'll grow between now and ten years from now, make an **Embarrassing Moments Time Capsule.**

1. Find an old shoebox.

2. Put your most embarrassing photo, a list of the most embarrassing things that have happened to you, a list of embarrassing things you hope *don't* happen to you in the next ten years, and a letter about yourself to your older self all inside the box. Also include a list of embarrassing pop culture stuff, like pictures of embarrassing celebrity moments from your favorite magazines, or newspaper articles about mistakes made by politicians or people in your town. Finally, write down the names of the people you currently consider your confidants—and remind yourself to look them up in ten years!

3. Seal the box with heavy-duty tape and write "Private!" on it.

4. Ask one of your parents to hold on to it for ten years or to give it to you when you graduate from college. Or tuck it away in the bottom of your closet, where you'll forget about it for the next decade!

```
T  E ( T  I  Z  R  E  T  S  N  O  M ) S  O
B  N  Y ( E  M  A  I  L  D  R  A  M  A ) T  P
A  I ( H  T  E  E  T  N  I  D  O  O  F ) A  E
D  A  P  O  M  F  O  B  A  B  R  P  A  N  E
B  T  S  I  N  L  R  N  L  I  M  E  R  I  M
R  S  T  E  N  I  K  I  I  K  P  N  T  I  O
E  D  S  T  R  I  K  K  Z  B  A  F  I  Z  N
A  O  E  N  A  T  K  E  T  Z  B  L  N  Z  T
T  I  F  O  O  J  J  L  E  H  Y  Y  C  N  T
H  R  S  C  H  Y  Z  Z  I  T  Y  H  L  I  F
P  E  R  I  O  X  F  O  O  P  R  S  A  Z  A
E  P  A ( T  U  O  E  K  I  R  T ) S  I  R
H  E  F  R  O  Z  Z  Y  O  U  T  Z  S  R  R
(I  N  I  K  I  B  G  N  I  S  S  I  M ) B  O
```

In Case of Emergency

HAVE U HEARD?

Remember that golden rule on page 13 about "Reaching Out" to people you *trust* when embarrassing moments strike?

Well, it's time to plan ahead. Make a list of the top 3–6 people who've proven to you that they're trustworthy, loyal, and neither competitive with nor jealous of you. (In other words, think of the people in your life who won't go blabbing about your situation.) They could be friends, siblings, parents, teachers . . . *anyone* who's helped you get through stuff before. Then, write down their phone number and e-mail address on this page, so you have it all in one place the next time you need it, and think of it as your Embarrassing Moment Yellow Pages!

NAME: NAME:

PHONE: PHONE:

EMAIL: EMAIL:

NAME: NAME:

PHONE: PHONE:

EMAIL: EMAIL:

NAME: NAME:

PHONE: PHONE:

EMAIL: EMAIL:

additional resources: the 411

Need help with a situation that goes *beyond* blushing?

Check out these websites and hotlines, and remember: No matter how overwhelmed you might feel sometimes, you're not alone. You can always talk to a trusted adult—a parent, school counselor, or family friend—about any issue that's on your mind, and additional confidential guidance is always just a phone call or click away.

FOR HELP WITH YOUR . . .
School & Homework:

Federal Citizen Information Center for Kids
www.kids.gov

U.S. Department of Education, Students' Page
www.ed.gov/students

FOR HELP WITH YOUR . . .
Relationships & Sexuality:

Planned Parenthood
www.teenwire.com

FOR HELP
WITH YOUR . . .
Health & Body:

BAM!, Body and Mind (from Centers for Disease Control
and Prevention)
www.bam.gov

GirlsHealth.gov
www.girlshealth.gov

TeensHealth
www.teenshealth.org

U.S. Food & Drug Administration (see information for teens)
www.fda.gov

FOR HELP WITH YOUR . . .
Miscellaneous & Emergency:

National Youth Violence Prevention Resource Center
www.safeyouth.org

The Partnership for a Drug-Free America
www.drugfree.org/teen

index